Also by Linda Cobb

A Queen for All Seasons

Talking Dirty Laundry with
the Queen of Clean®

Talking Dirty with the Queen of Clean®

The Queen of Clean®

THE ROYAL GUIDE TO
SPOT AND STAIN REMOVAL

Linda Cobb

POCKET BOOKS
New York   London   Toronto   Sydney   Singapore

POCKET BOOKS, a division of Simon & Schuster, Inc.
1230 Avenue of the Americas, New York, NY 10020

Copyright © 2001 by Linda Cobb

Excerpted from *Talking Dirty with the Queen of Clean®* copyright © 1998 by Linda Cobb and *Talking Dirty Laundry with the Queen of Clean®* copyright © 2001 by Linda Cobb

ISBN: 0-7434-3783-7

First Pocket Books mass market paperback printing November 2001

10 9 8 7 6 5 4 3 2 1

Queen of Clean® is the registered trademark of Linda Cobb and is the property of Queen and King Enterprises, Inc.

POCKET and colophon are registered trademarks of Simon & Schuster, Inc.

For information regarding special discounts for bulk purchases, please contact Simon & Schuster Special Sales at 1-800-456-6798 or business@simonandschuster.com

Cover photo credits: author photo by John Hall; other photos by Siede Preis/GettyOne, Eyewire Collection/GettyOne, Thierry Dosogne/Image Bank, Bob Winsett/Index Stock Imagery

Interior illustrations by Jeff Jones

Book designed by Helene Berinsky

Printed in the U.S.A.

This book is dedicated to my Mom and Dad, Cecil and Florine Conway.

Because of them I can fly . . .
on very clean wings!

CONTENTS

INTRODUCTION

You're ready to leave the house in the morning when you notice a nice big coffee stain in the middle of your brand-new blouse.

That romantic candlelit dinner has left you with wax on your grandmother's tablecloth.

Your favorite pants come out of the wash with a strange black splotch in the shape of Michigan.

Junior's just come home with a first-place ribbon—and a great big grass stain.

That "absorbent, non-greasy" hand cream has just been absorbed into your skirt!

You hear: "Do you want fries with that?" and think "ketchup stain."

Stains happen! They happen to the best of us, and they happen all the time. Doesn't matter how careful you are, doesn't matter how clean. All it takes is a slip of a spoon, a wayward French fry, a leaky pen, or dirty bus seat to ruin your favorite clothes. But it doesn't have to be that way. A stain doesn't necessarily mean ruin . . . not if you approach it the right way.

The most important thing to remember about stain removal is that you have to consider the fabric as well as the stain. You can't treat silk as you would denim. You can't be as vigorous with a lace blouse as you would with a cotton tee. That's first. The second thing to bear in mind is that not all stains are created equal. Chocolate requires a different remedy from wine. The solution for ink wouldn't work on grass stains—and gum requires a treatment all its own.

That said, I'd like to encourage a little creativity in your stain removal repertoire. Don't reach for the same old product every time. Especially if it doesn't work. (Be careful of using stain removers that contain repellents, though. If the stain doesn't come out the first time, the repellent could lock it in and you could be marked for life. Not a pretty prospect.) Take a look in your cupboard. You'll be surprised at the great stain removers you'll find there, things like alcohol, baking soda, glycerin, and salt. And after you get used to using these items *as is*, you can be a little adventurous and make your own natural products. These homemade remedies are fun to concoct. They cost less than their store-bought counterparts and are better for the environment too. Give them a try. You may never go back.

So relax. Here is my *all you need to know* Royal Spot and Stain Removal Guide, straight from the Palace. Once you've read my Royal Rules of Stain Removal—and you will, won't you—you're well on your way to getting off spot free!

Royal Rules of Stain Removal

• Test the spot remover on hidden or inconspicuous areas of the fabric before you proceed.

• Approach the stain from the "wrong" side of the fabric. Put a pad of paper toweling under the offending spot as you work. This will help to blot the stain.

• Always blot, never rub! Rubbing will spread the spot and harm the fabric.

• Do not iron or apply heat to spots or stains. Heat will set the stain and you will never be able to remove it.

• If you don't know what caused the stain, start with the weakest and simplest stain removal method.

• Make sure to consider the fabric as well as the stain.

• Remember, the faster you react to a spill

or a spot, the better your chances are of removing it completely.

- Directing a blow-dryer at a freshly blotted spot will help it to dry without a ring.

- Sometimes you may still need to pretreat using your favorite laundry spotter, such as Zout®.

Part I

. . . .

STAIN REMOVERS

1

Stain Removers That Are Hiding in Your Cupboard

Some of the very best spot and stain removers are things you use every single day! These stain removers work great and they're right at your fingertips!

Alcohol: Rubbing alcohol is great for grass stains and so much more.

Ammonia: The perspiration stain fighter.

Automatic dishwasher detergent: Keep this

on hand as a bleach substitute and whitener/ brightener even if you *don't* have a dish-washer. Liquid, powder, and tablet form all work well. If you choose the tablet, make sure it has dissolved before you add clothes. Pour directly on stain, or soak.

Baking soda: Removes odors.

Club soda: My favorite *Oh my gosh, how did I do that?* spotter. Use it on any fabric or surface that can be treated with water. A slight dabbing on dry-clean-only fabrics is also permissible, just be sure to test first! Use club soda on any spill—ask the waiter for some if you're dining out—dab it on and blot it off. Club soda keeps spills from becoming stains and brings the offending spill to the surface so it can be easily removed. It's totally safe. I always make sure to have a bottle on hand.

Cream of tartar: I bet you have some of this in the kitchen cupboard, but how often do you use it? Well, here's your chance. Mix cream of tartar with lemon juice and you have a wonderful bleach for white clothes spotted with food or other stains. It's even effective on many rust stains.

Denture-cleaning tablets: The cure-all for white table linens with food stains and white cotton with stains. Dissolve one tablet per ½ cup water. Pour directly on stain or spot.

Dishwashing liquid: A wonderful spotter, used undiluted on tough stains.

Glycerin: You can remove tar, tree sap (think Christmas tree), juice stains, mustard, ketchup and barbecue sauce.

GOJO Crème Waterless Hand Cleaner®: Totally awesome for removing grease and oil, including shoe polish.

Hydrogen peroxide: 3 percent hydrogen peroxide is super for removing bloodstains, especially if they are fairly fresh. It also is a wonderful bleaching agent for stubborn stains on white clothes. Combine ½ cup of hydrogen peroxide and 1 teaspoon of ammonia for an unbeatable stain removal combination. Make sure to use 3 percent and *not* the kind you use to bleach your hair!

Lemon juice: This is nature's bleach and disinfectant. I don't know where we'd be without it. If you have spots on white clothes, apply some lemon juice and lay them in the sun. Apply a little more lemon juice prior to laundering, or prespray and launder as usual. This is really effective on baby formula stains.

Meat tenderizer: A combo of meat tenderizer (unseasoned, please, or you'll have a whole new stain!) and cold water is just the answer to protein-based stains such as blood, milk, etc.

Salt: Sprinkling salt on spilled red wine will keep the wine from staining until you can launder it. Mixed with lemon juice, salt will remove mildew stains.

Shampoo: Any brand will do. Cheap is fine. I save the small bottles from hotel/motel stays and keep them in the laundry room. Great for treating ring-around-the-collar, mud and cosmetic stains.

Shave cream: That innocent-looking can of shave cream in your bathroom is one of the best spot and stain removers available. That's because it's really whipped soap! If you have a spill on your clothes (or even your carpet), moisten the spot, work in some shave cream, and then flush it with cool water. If the offending spot is on something you're wearing, work the shave cream in and then use a clean cloth (a washcloth works fine) to blot the shave cream and the spot away. A quick touch of the blow-dryer to prevent a ring and you're on your way. The best thing about shave cream is that even if it doesn't work it won't set the stain, so the spot can still be removed later. Keep a small sample can in your suitcase when you travel. It's saved me more than once!

WD-40 Lubricant®: Check out your garage or the "fix-it" cupboard. If you don't have any, pick up a can the next time you're at the hardware store or home center. Why? Because we've all had those nasty grease stains and oil stains on clothes: Salad dressing misses the salad and gets the blouse, or grease splatters when you are cooking—or crayon/lipstick/ Chap Stick® gets on your clothes! WD-40 is your answer. Spray some on, wait 10 minutes, and then work in undiluted liquid dishwashing soap and launder as usual. Works well on everything *except* silk!

White vinegar: A great spotter for suede— used undiluted. It's also a wonderful fabric softener. Just put ¼ cup white vinegar in the final rinse. (And no, you won't smell like a salad!)

It's worthwhile to keep these things on hand. As you can see, most are inexpensive *and* have other uses. They'll make you the laundry Queen—or King!—in your home.

2

Be a Spot
Hot Shot!

I love natural products, and I love things that I can make for pennies and still have them work better than the products I could buy at the store. Here are some of my favorite laundry spot removers. Use them just as you would over-the-counter products, but take note: many of them are designed to take care of specific spots and stains.

Start with a clean spray and/or squeeze

bottle, and always be sure to label any product you make. It's important to know what the bottle contains and what it was intended for. I like to include the recipe on the label too—that way I can mix up additional product with ease. Cover the label with clear packaging tape or a piece of clear adhesive sheet to protect the label from moisture.

These spotters are all intended for washable fabrics. If in doubt, test in an inconspicuous spot, such as a seam.

General All-Purpose Laundry Spotter

Combine the following to make a generic spotter that works on a wide variety of stains:

1 part rubbing alcohol

2 parts water

If you use a large spray bottle you can add 1 bottle of alcohol and 2 of the alcohol bottles filled with water. Spray this on spots and spills, wait a few minutes, and then launder as usual.

Beverage, Fruit and Grass Remover

Combine equal portions of:

white vinegar
liquid dishwashing soap
water

Shake well and work the solution into the spot. Let stand a few minutes and then launder as usual.

Non-oily Stain Remover

Combine equal portions of the following ingredients:

ammonia
liquid dishwashing soap
water

Shake well, and work the solution into the spot. Let stand a few minutes and flush with water. This solution works well on stains such as milk, blood, perspiration and urine. *Do not use on washable wool, silk, spandex, acrylic and acetate.*

Oily Stain Remover

Combine the following:

1 tablespoon glycerin
1 tablespoon liquid dishwashing soap
8 tablespoons of water

Work the solution into grease and oil stains. Let sit a few minutes, flush with water, and launder as usual.

Again, remember all of these spotters are for washable fabrics only and none of them are for silk, wool, spandex, acrylic and acetate. When in doubt, test first!

3

Bringing Out
the Big Guns

I t's time to talk about the big guns of laundry spotters. We all need them from time to time. But what's best? What really works? Read on. I've tried them all, so you won't have to!

A quick disclaimer: Remember, I am counting on you to test a small, inconspicuous area on the fabric for colorfastness *before* you use any of these spotters. Don't let laundry spotters dry. Launder soon after spotting to prevent the spot from becoming a stain. Don't let me down!

Energine Cleaning Fluid®: This is a terrific "can't be without" spotter for dry-clean-only clothes. Blot it on until the stain is gone and then blow-dry to avoid a ring.

Fels-Naptha Heavy Duty Laundry Bar Soap®: This is that old-fashioned brown bar soap that your grandmother used. It has been around 100 years—literally!—and it's a great spotter for numerous spots and stains. Wet the bar and simply rub the stain, working it in well. Let it sit a few minutes. This spotter still works even if allowed to dry on the fabric. Great for ring-around-the-collar and perspiration stains.

Ink Away™: Ink and marker can be a challenge to remove, but this product, made by the makers of Goo Gone™, really proves its worth. Follow package directions carefully and be sure to read the list of things *not* to use it on *before* you start.

Spot Shot® Instant Carpet Stain Remover: This one wins the prize for the most unusual laundry spotter, but it's *still* one of the Queen's favorite products. Yes, that's right, it's not just for carpet. It's also a great laundry prewash spotter—and boy does it work. It is safe for all colorfast washables and works in all wash temperatures. Spray the stained area thoroughly, saturating the stain. If the stain is difficult or stubborn, work it between your thumbs. Allow Spot Shot® to sit at least 60 seconds, and then launder as usual. *Do not* allow it to dry on the fabric and do not use it on silks, fabrics labeled "dry clean only" or noncolorfast fabrics. This product works on oily stains, ink, pet stains, cola, shoe polish, lipstick, blood and others. A must-have in the laundry room.

Wine Away Red Wine Stain Remover™: Don't let the name fool you, this product is much more than a red wine stain remover. It works great on Kool-Aid™, grape juice, red pop, cranberry juice, orange pop, coffee and tea, as well as red wine. I even took red food coloring out of a shirt with it. Wine Away™ is made from fruit and vegetable extracts and is totally nontoxic—I love that!

Zout® Stain Remover: This is a super-concentrated stain remover that works great on ink, blood, grease, fruit juice, grass and hundreds of other stains. A little goes a long way with this. Simply saturate the stain, work it in, wait 5 to 10 minutes, and then launder as usual.

4

Bleach 101:
Whiter Whites, Brighter
Brights

Are you one of those people who thinks that directions are what you read to find out what you did wrong? Then pay attention. I'm going to give you my dos and don'ts of bleach basics.

DO ....

• **Read the directions on the container of bleach.**

- Check the labels on the fabric you wish to bleach.

- Test the bleach if you are unsure. To do this with chlorine bleach, mix 1 tablespoon of chlorine bleach with ¼ cup of cold water. Find a hidden area on the piece of clothing and place a drop of the solution on it. Leave this for a minute or two and then blot to determine if there is any color change.

- To test all-fabric bleaches, mix 1 teaspoon of the bleach with 1 cup of hot water. Again, place a drop on an inconspicuous area. Wait at least 15 minutes, blot, and check for any change in the color.

- Of course if any color change takes place you won't want to use that type of bleach on that type of fabric.

- Always be sure to rinse bleach out of fabric thoroughly.

DON'TS

- Absolutely never allow undiluted chlorine bleach to come in contact with fabrics.

- **Never use any kind of bleach directly on fabric without testing it first.**

- **Never use more bleach than called for. It can damage fabrics and is wasteful too.**

- *NEVER* **use chlorine bleach and ammonia in the same wash! It can generate deadly fumes.**

Now let's talk about the bleaches one by one.

Chlorine Bleach

The strongest, fastest-acting bleach available, chlorine bleach is very effective on cottons, linens, and some synthetics when used properly. Used improperly it can weaken cloth fibers, causing them to disintegrate. It can even cause holes. Always follow container directions with care, and never use chlorine bleach on silk, wool, spandex, acetate, fibers treated to be flame-resistant or dry-clean-only fabrics.

Most of us have had a bad experience with chlorine bleach, so use care. Never pour it on hand washables, and never pour it onto clothes that are in the washing machine. Pour it in the bleach dispenser, if your washing machine is so equipped, or into the washer while it is filling with water *before* adding the clothes. For hand washables, dilute it prior to adding the clothes and be sure to adjust the amount accordingly for the amount of water being used.

Name brands and store brands work the same, so purchase the product of your choice, or the one with the best price.

All-Fabric Bleach or Oxygen Bleach

This is a much milder form of bleach that works well on delicate fabrics or those requiring gentle care. It is slower-acting than chlorine bleach and is less effective in restoring whiteness to fabrics. It may be effective, though, through regular use. This bleach can be used on all fabrics, even silks, as long as the manufacturer's care tag does not say "no bleach." Add this bleach at the same time you add your detergent and do not pour directly on the clothes. More is not better, so measure; don't just pour.

A New Generation of Bleach

Soapworks® has come up with a new generation of bleach that is effective, user friendly, and safe for use by people with allergies and asthma. It is hypoallergenic, nontoxic, biodegradable, 100 percent natural, safe for septic tanks, contains no chemicals, no dyes and no fragrances.

This product is called Brilliant™, and it is just that! Created with hydrogen peroxide—which is the safest, natural whitener and brightener for fabrics—this bleach can be used effectively on whites and colored fabrics both. Clothes can be soaked safely for 24 hours or more without harm to either fabric or color.

Brilliant™ is also a softener, so no additional softening agent is required. Add ¼ cup to the washer as it fills with water. As with any bleach product, test in an inconspicuous area when in doubt.

Making Your Own Bleaching Agents

Yes, you *can* create your own forms of bleach with things you already have at home.

Lemon juice: Nature's bleach and disinfectant, lemon juice can be used to whiten clothes.

Take 1 gallon of the hottest water possible for the fabric you're bleaching and add ½ cup of bottled lemon juice or the slices of one or two lemons. Soak the clothes for 30 minutes or even overnight. This works especially well on white socks and underwear, and is safe for polyester fabrics. Don't use on silks, though.

Automatic dishwasher detergent: This is another wonderful bleaching agent for white clothes. Fill a bucket with the hottest possible water for the fabric you are working with, and add 2 tablespoons of any brand of automatic dishwasher detergent. Soak white clothes for 30 minutes or even overnight. Dump into the washer and launder with your detergent as usual.

To use this bleaching technique in the washer, fill the machine with water and add ¼ cup to ½ cup of automatic dishwasher detergent. Agitate for several minutes and then add clothes. Soak as directed above and then add detergent and launder as usual.

Hydrogen peroxide: This can be used to

bleach delicate items such as wool or wool blends. Soak them overnight in a solution of 1 part 3 percent hydrogen peroxide to 8 parts cold water. Launder according to care directions.

Bluing

Bluing is a whitening and brightening agent that has been around for a long, long time. Available in liquid form, bluing contains blue pigment, which actually counteracts the yellowing that occurs in some fabrics. Always dilute this with water as directed on the bottle, and never pour directly on clothes or spill on other fibers or surfaces. Look for it in the laundry aisle at the grocery store. This product will even remove the yellow from gray hair!

Part II

. . . .

CLEANING GUIDE
FOR FABRIC TYPES

Yes, it's true. I really am "stain stalker." And in these next pages I am going to walk you through laundry procedures for certain fabric types and unusual items.

Acetate: This is a temperamental fabric. Do not allow it to become heavily soiled and do not use an enzyme detergent when laundering. Acetate is commonly used for curtains, brocades, taffetas, and satin. (Think evening wear.) It's also a popular lining. You can machine wash acetate in cold water or you can hand wash. Be sure not to spin or wring acetate as this will set wrinkles. Rinse extremely well and press with a cool (low setting) iron on the "wrong" side of the fabric.

Acrylic: This fabric should be laundered frequently since it can retain perspiration odors. Acrylic is usually machine washable in cool water. Check the care label. Dry flat or hang to dry, being sure to reshape the garment while it is still damp.

Angora: This wool is made from rabbit fur or goat hair. Angora sheds a lot, although if it's blended with nylon it will shed less. Wash angora in warm or cool water using a very mild soap or a little shampoo. Do not rub, twist, or lift the garment up and down in the water as this will cause stretching. Washing in a sink is best. Let the water run out and then press the liquid out of the garment. Rinse well again, pressing the water out. Roll the garment in a towel and then reshape. Dry flat out of the sun. Do not press—instead, hold a steam iron just above the garment to remove wrinkles.

Blends: Blends, such as cotton/polyester, are made from combined fibers. To launder these fabrics, follow the guidelines for the most delicate or the most prominent fiber. The most common blends are cotton/polyester, cotton/linen, and silk/polyester.

Brocades: Use care when laundering brocades. You don't want to crush or flatten the pile design. Hand wash in cool water or dry-clean according to the care label. Do not wring. Iron on the "wrong" side using a press cloth or towel between the fabric and the iron.

Canvas: A heavy, firm, very tightly woven fabric, canvas was originally made from cotton or linen, but now it comes in synthetics or blends. Machine wash canvas in cold water and tumble dry on a low setting. Test for colorfastness before washing. If it's not colorfast, have it dry-cleaned.

Cashmere: This is an expensive fiber that

comes from the undercoat of cashmere goats. Treat it with respect. Dry-clean these prizes or hand wash with care in cool water and well-dissolved gentle soap. Rinse well and do not wring. Dry flat, reshaping the garment as it dries. Iron on the "wrong" side while still damp with a cool iron, if necessary.

Chiffon: This is a very thin, transparent fabric, made from silk or synthetic fibers. Hand wash as you would silk.

Chintz: Glazed cotton, and often printed. Dry-clean this fabric unless the label states that it can be washed. Follow the care label instructions carefully.

Corduroy: Take care when washing corduroy. It wears well, but care is needed to avoid crushing and distorting the pile. Turn corduroy inside out and launder using warm water. Dry at a normal setting. Remove from the dryer while still damp and smooth the seams, pockets, etc. Hang to complete drying, and iron on the "wrong" side of the fabric. Pile may be restored by brushing gently.

Cotton: This natural vegetable fiber is woven and knitted into fabrics in all weights and textures. Hand wash lightweight fabrics such as organdy and batiste and hang to air dry. Iron when damp with a hot iron.

Machine wash light-colored and white medium to heavyweight cottons in warm water. Use cold water for bright colors that may bleed. Dry on a low dryer setting. Remove from the dryer while still damp and iron with a hot iron right away.

Damask: This is a jacquard-weave fabric. It may be made of cotton, linen, silk, wool or a blend. Hand wash lightweight fabrics and be sure to check the individual fiber listings. Dry-clean silk, wool and all heavier weight fabrics.

Denim: If you have jeans, you know this strong fabric is prone to shrinking, streaking and fading. Machine wash denim in warm water. Blue and other deep colors bleed the first several washings, so be sure to wash separately. Washing older, faded jeans with the new ones will restore some of their original color.

Dry at low settings to avoid shrinkage. Iron while damp if necessary and be aware that jeans may bleed color onto your ironing board.

Down: Down is the soft underfeather of waterfowl that is often combined with adult feathers. It is machine washable *and* dry-cleanable. Just be sure to follow the care label closely. Much of the treatment will depend on the fabric covering the down, so pay attention to manufacturer's directions.

Do not air-dry down. It dries too slowly and mold or mildew may form in the process. Dry in your dryer, using a large capacity dryer if need be. Set temperatures low (under 140 degrees), fluffing and turning the item often. Make sure to dry the item thoroughly. This can take time.

Want really fluffy duvets and pillows? Putting a clean tennis shoe or tennis ball in with the item will fluff it up!

Flannel: Flannel is actually a napped fabric, and it comes in a plain or twill-type weave. Cotton and synthetics should be washed according to the care label, but when in doubt, use cool water and mild detergent. Dry at a low dryer setting and remove flannel while damp to avoid wrinkles. You may also line-dry this fabric. Wool flannel should be dry-cleaned.

Gabardine: Firm, tightly woven twill fabric, often worsted wool, but sometimes made of cotton and synthetic fibers. We are seeing a large amount of synthetic fibers sold as gabardine in trousers and blazers for men and women. Follow your label directions—many synthetics are machine washable and dryable. If the care label says dry-clean, be sure to do so.

Lace: An extremely delicate fabric, lace may be made of cotton, linen or synthetic. Wash using a mild soap or detergent intended for delicates. Avoid rubbing since it will distort the fibers. Rinse well without wringing, shape by hand, and hang to air-dry or dry flat. Delicate lace pieces may need to be reshaped and pinned down to dry. If you must iron lace, do so over a terrycloth towel. (White is best.) Never put lace in the dryer.

Leather and suede: Generally, leather and suede are not washable. Check your care label carefully. If you have washable leather items, wash them by hand and be sure to protect them with a leather spray protectant. To clean suede, rub it with another piece of suede or a suede brush (not any other kind of brush) to restore the nap and keep it looking new.

Remember, leather needs to breathe, so do not cover it with plastic or store in a tightly enclosed area. If you are looking for a dust cover for leather or suede, use cloth—an old pillowcase is ideal.

To remove spots from leather (not for suede), try using cuticle remover. Rub it into the spot, wait 10 minutes, and then massage the area with a cloth dipped in the cuticle remover. Wipe down thoroughly.

To remove spots from suede, try dabbing with white vinegar.

Linen: A tough fabric that withstands high temperatures, linen is a favorite in hot climates. It is made of natural flax fiber, and comes in light to heavyweight fabrics. Hand wash or machine wash linen in warm water (again, read your care label). If the fabric is colorfast you may remove stains and brighten the fabric with an oxygen bleach or Brilliant Bleach™ from Soapworks®. Do not use chlorine bleach.

Iron while still damp, and to help prevent creasing you may treat with starch or sizing. Press heavyweight linens with a hot iron, and for lighter weight linen and blends (linen, plus other fibers), iron with a warm iron.

Linen is also dry-cleanable.

Mohair: An oldie but a goodie! This is fiber taken from angora goats. Follow the directions for cleaning wool.

Nylon: This is a durable synthetic fiber that comes in varying weights and is often blended with other fibers. When used alone it is machine washable in warm water. It can also be cleaned.

Dry on a low setting or hang to dry using a nonmetal hanger. Do not dry in sunlight— that will cause yellowing. Nonchlorine bleach is best for nylon.

Organdy: Think party dress! Sheer and

lightweight, organdy is actually a cotton fiber. Hand wash this and iron damp with a hot iron. Use starch as you iron to give it a crisp look. May also be dry-cleaned.

Polyester: This strong synthetic fiber won't stretch or shrink, which is probably why it's so popular. It comes in various weights and textures, and is often found blended with cotton and wool.

Wash polyester in warm water. Tumble dry and make sure not to let it sit in the dryer, because that will encourage wrinkles. Remove it immediately and you may not need to iron it. If ironing *is* necessary, make sure to use a low setting.

If the polyester is blended with another fiber, just follow the washing instructions for the more delicate fiber.

Ramie: Very similar to linen, ramie is a natural fiber made from—what else—the ramie plant! It can be used alone or blended with other fibers, such as ramie/cotton.

Machine wash in warm water, tumble dry, and iron while damp with a hot iron. Avoid twisting the fibers or they will become distorted. May be dry-cleaned also.

Rayon: This is a synthetic fiber that is sometimes called "viscose." Follow the care label directions closely, but for the very best results, have this fabric dry-cleaned. Dry-cleaning not only cleans well, but it gives rayon the crisp pressing it needs to maintain its shape and good looks.

Satin: Originally made only from silk, this shiny fabric is available in acetate, cotton, nylon, and even polyester.

Dry-clean satin made out of silk and acetate. You may wash cotton, nylon and polyester satins, as long as you follow the washing instructions for those fibers.

Seersucker: You've seen this fabric in shirts, blouses and nightwear. It has puckered stripes that are woven in during the manufacturing process. Seersucker is most frequently made of cotton, but it's also available in nylon and polyester. Be guided by the fiber content for washing and drying.

Drip-dry or tumble dry and iron on low heat if necessary.

Silk: This is a natural fiber made by the silkworm. It is a delicate fabric that requires special care to avoid damage. Check the care labels, but you may be able to hand wash crepe de chine, thin, lightweight and medium weight silk in lukewarm water with mild soap or detergent. You can also use cold water with cold water detergent.

Do not use chlorine bleach. You may use Brilliant Bleach™ by Soapworks without damaging the fibers.

Rinsing silk well is important. Rinse several times in cold water to remove all suds. Towel blot and dry flat. Do not wring or rub silk.

Iron on the "wrong" side of the fabric with a warm iron.

If your care label indicates that the garment is machine washable, follow the directions with the utmost care. Dry cleaning works best for suits, pleated silks, and silks that are not colorfast.

Do not use strong spotters or enzyme spotters on silk.

Spandex: Spandex is added to other fibers to give them stretch and elasticity. Machine wash in warm water on the delicate or gentle cycle. Do not use chlorine bleach. Do not put them in the dryer, or iron; high heat will break down spandex fibers. Line-dry or dry flat, per care label.

If you have exercise clothes containing spandex, be sure to launder each time you wear them. Body oil can break down spandex fibers.

Swimwear: After swimming in a chlorinated pool, soak your suit for 15 minutes or so in cold water with a little liquid fabric softener. Rinse in cold water, then wash in cool water with mild detergent. Rinse well again and dry in the shade. Chlorine is very hard on fabrics, weakening them and changing the color, so be sure to rinse the suit as soon as you can. Never put your suit away without rinsing it out first.

If the suit has been worn in saltwater, soak it for a few minutes in cold water to remove the salt, then wash in cold water with mild detergent. Rinse well and dry in the shade.

Fold the suit in shape once it's dry. Store in tissue or in a perforated plastic bag for winter. (A perforated bag will allow the fabric to breathe.)

Terry cloth: A toweling-type of fabric, terry cloth has a looped pile made of cotton or cotton/polyester blend. You find it in towels, of course, and even sleepwear.

Machine wash in warm or hot water. Tumble or line dry. Add softener for a softer texture.

Velour: This is a napped fabric that is available in wool, cotton, silk and synthetics. Dry-clean unless the care label indicates it can be washed and dried.

Velvet: A beautiful soft pile fabric, velvet comes in silk, rayon or cotton. Dry-clean for best results.

To raise the pile on velvet, steam from the "wrong" side over a pot of boiling water. Hold the fabric at least 12 inches from the water, and be careful not to allow the fabric to come in contact with the water. This works well for creases in the back of dresses, etc.

Wool: This is a natural fiber made from the fleece of sheep. Hand wash sweaters and other knits in cold water with cold water detergent. Rinse several times and do not wring or twist.

Towel blot and dry flat, reshaping as needed.

Part III

. . . .

A TO Z PALACE
SPOT AND STAIN
REMOVAL GUIDE

ACID: Acid can permanently damage fabrics, so it must be treated immediately. Neutralize acid by flushing the area with cold running water as soon as possible. Next, spread the garment over a pad of paper towels and moisten with ammonia. Dab the spot several times, then flush again with cold water. If you do not have ammonia on hand, apply a paste of cold water and baking soda, then flush with water. Repeat this several times, then launder as usual.

Do not use undiluted ammonia on wool or silk, or on any blends containing these fibers. If you have acid on silk or wool you may dilute ammonia with equal parts of cold water and apply as directed above.

ADHESIVE TAPE: Sponge adhesive tape with eucalyptus oil, baby oil, or cooking oil. Allow to soak 10 minutes or so, then work in undiluted dishwashing liquid and rinse well. Pretreat and launder as usual.

You may also consider using De-Solv-it™, Goo Gone™, or Un-Du™ to remove adhesives from fabric and hard surfaces. Un-Du™ is so great it will remove a stamp from an envelope!

ALCOHOLIC BEVERAGES: These stains will turn brown with age, so it is important to treat them as soon as possible. First, flush the area with cold water or with club soda, then sponge immediately with a cloth barely dampened with warm water and 1 or 2 drops of liquid dish soap. Rinse with cool water and dry the area with a hair dryer set on medium.

Alcohol is often invisible when it is spilled, but it can oxidize with heat and age, which makes it impossible to remove. Presoak dry alcohol stains in an enzyme solution such as Biz All Fabric Bleach™, and launder as usual.

If you spill alcohol on a dry-clean-only fabric, sponge with cold water or club soda and then take the garment to the dry cleaner as soon as possible. Make sure to point out the stain.

For beer spills, sponge with a solution of equal parts white vinegar and dishwashing liquid, then rinse in warm water.

For treating red and white wine spills, see **Wine.**

ANIMAL HAIR: Removing pet hair from clothes and bedding can be a challenge. Try using a damp sponge and wiping over clothes and bedding, etc. Rinse the sponge frequently to keep it clean. You can also remove hair by putting on rubber gloves and dipping them in water. Simply dip and wipe, dip and wipe. The hair will rinse off easily.

ANTIPERSPIRANTS AND DEODORANTS: Antiperspirants that contain aluminum chloride are acidic and may interact with some fabrics. If color changes have occurred, try sponging fabric with ammonia. Rinse thoroughly, and remember to dilute ammonia with equal portions of water when spotting wool or silk.

If you want to avoid yellow underarm stains and prevent color removal, take a bar of Fels-Naptha Soap® and work it into the underarm of clothes *before* you launder them for the first time, even if you see no visible stain. Work up a good lather between your thumbs and then launder as usual.

You can also try applying rubbing alcohol to the stain and covering the area with a folded paper towel dampened with alcohol. Keep it moist and let it sit for a few hours prior to laundering.

To treat yellowed areas that have become stiff, apply an enzyme-soaking product. Biz All Fabric Bleach™ is a good one to try. Make a stiff paste of the powder by mixing it with cold water. Rub it into the stained areas. Next, put the garment in a plastic bag and leave 8 hours or overnight. Wash in very hot water. If dealing with fabrics that can't withstand hot water, drape the underarm area over a sink and pour 1 quart of hot water through the fabric. Launder as usual.

Don't iron over a deodorant stain or you will never be able to remove it.

I have also had success soaking garments with underarm stains in a solution of 1 quart warm water and 3 tablespoons of Brilliant Bleach™. Soak up to several days if necessary. Brilliant Bleach™ is safe for whites and color-fast garments.

Last-ditch effort: Spray the stained area heavily with heated white vinegar, work in 20 Mule Team® Borax, roll up in a plastic bag and leave overnight, then launder as usual.

BABY FORMULA: For white clothes, try applying lemon juice to the stains and laying the garment in the sun. Pretreat and launder as usual.

Unseasoned meat tenderizer is also great for removing formula and baby food stains. Make a paste of the tenderizer and cool water, rub it into the stain, and let sit for an hour or so before laundering. Meat tenderizer contains an enzyme that breaks down protein stains. Just make sure to use *unseasoned* tenderizer.

Soaking colored clothes and whites in Brilliant Bleach™ is also effective, although you may have to soak for several days to achieve perfect results on difficult stains. Remember, this bleach is nonchlorine, so it's totally safe for baby things.

BARBEQUE SAUCE: See *Tomato-Based Stains.*

BERRIES (blueberries, cranberries, raspberries, strawberries): There are many complex ways to deal with berry stains, but I've had great success with one of the simplest, a product called Wine Away Red Wine Stain Remover™. Don't be fooled by the name, it works on red fruit stains and juices too.

Just spray Wine Away™ straight on the fabric and watch in amazement as it breaks down the stain. Follow the directions on the con-

Talking Dirty Laundry
with the
Queen of Clean·

OFFICIAL MAIL-IN REBATE OFFER FORM

To receive your 50¢ REBATE CHECK by mail:

- Purchase the paperback edition of Linda Cobb's *Talking Dirty Laundry with the Queen of Clean®* by February 1, 2002.
- Mail this official form (no photocopies accepted) and the original store cash register receipt for *Talking Dirty Laundry with the Queen of Clean®* dated on or before February 1, 2002, with the purchase price circled.

A QUEEN FOR ALL SEASONS

OFFICIAL MAIL-IN REBATE OFFER FORM

To receive your 50¢ REBATE CHECK by mail:

- Purchase the paperback edition of Linda Cobb's *A Queen for All Seasons* by February 1, 2002.
- Mail this official form (no photocopies accepted) and the original store cash register receipt for *A Queen for All Seasons* dated on or before February 1, 2002, with the purchase price circled.

...er carefully and launder immediately after
...Totally nontoxic, Wine Away™ is safe on
all washable surfaces.

BEVERAGES: Blot beverage spills immediately
until you have absorbed all you can, then
sponge with clean, warm water and a little
borax. (About ½ teaspoon borax to ½ cup of
water.) Sponge and blot repeatedly and launder as usual.

Also see information under specific beverage stains.

BLOOD (fresh and dried): If you have blood all
over your clothes, laundry may not be your
biggest problem . . . for those little accidents
try the following:

For washable fabrics, soak as soon as possible in salt water or flush with club soda. You
can also make a paste of unseasoned meat tenderizer and cold water, and apply it to the
stain for a few hours. Wash in cool water and
detergent, by hand or machine.

Pouring 3 percent hydrogen peroxide
through the stained area can be effective in
many instances. The sooner you do this the

more success you will have. Make sure to do this only on washable fabrics, please. Pour the peroxide through the stain, then flush with cold water, pretreat and launder as usual.

Biz All Fabric Bleach™ and Brilliant Bleach™ both work well on blood. When using Biz™, make a paste with cold water and apply to the stain, allowing it to sit for several hours. With Brilliant Bleach™, soak the garment for a significant period of time—anywhere between 1 to 24 hours. Neither of these products will harm colorfast fabrics.

For dry-clean-only fabrics, sprinkle with salt while the blood is still moist, then take to a dry cleaner as soon as possible.

Human saliva will break down fresh bloodstains, so try applying a little of your own saliva to a small spot of blood—this may do the trick.

For a quick fix for fresh bloodstains, apply cornstarch to the surface and then flush from the "wrong" side of the fabric with soapy water. Pretreat and launder as usual.

Blood on leather can be foamed away with 3 percent hydrogen peroxide. Dab on the peroxide. Let it bubble and then blot. Continue until the blood is removed. Wipe the surface with a damp cloth and dry.

BUTTER OR MARGARINE: Scrape off any solid concentration of butter with a dull edge, such as the back of a knife.

On washable fabrics, work in undiluted dishwashing liquid, wash and dry.

If the stain is old, spray it with WD-40 Lubricant® to regenerate the grease, then work in undiluted dishwashing liquid and wash in the hottest water possible for that fabric type.

Sponge silks and delicate fabrics with Energine Cleaning Fluid®. Allow to air-dry. Repeat if necessary.

Do not iron the fabric until all traces of the grease have been removed. Ironing will set the stain and make it impossible to remove.

Take dry-clean-only fabrics to the dry cleaner as soon as possible. Be sure to identify the stain and its location on the garment.

CANDLE WAX: For candle wax on clothes and table linens, place the article in a plastic bag, place the bag in the freezer, and let the wax freeze. Scrape off what you can with a dull, straight edge—the back of a knife or an old credit card works well. Lay a brown paper bag, with no writing facing the fabric, on the ironing board. (Grocery store bags work well. Just make sure that the writing is face down on the ironing board *away* from the fabric—otherwise you may transfer lettering to your garment.) Cover with a similar bag (again, with the writing *away* from the fabric) and press with a medium/hot iron, moving the paper bag like a blotter until you have absorbed every bit of wax you can. Be patient! Blot with Energine Cleaning Fluid® to remove the balance of the grease from the wax.

Wieman Wax Away™ also works beautifully on any kind of wax. Follow the directions with care.

CANDY: To remove candy from fabrics, combine 1 tablespoon of liquid dish soap with 1 tablespoon of white vinegar and 1 quart of warm water. Soak the stain in it for 15 to 30 minutes, then flush with warm, clear water. Pretreat and launder as usual.

For chocolate stains, see *Chocolate.*

CHEWING GUM: See *Gum.*

CHOCOLATE: Scrape off all that you can, then soak washable fabrics for 30 minutes in an enzyme prewash solution such as Biz™. Rub detergent into any remaining stain and work well between your thumbs. Rinse the area under forcefully running cold water. If a grease spot remains, sponge the area with dry-cleaning solution such as Energine Cleaning Fluid®. Any residual stain should come out during normal washing. If the stain is still visible after washing, soak in Brilliant Bleach™ or combine ½ cup of 3 percent hydrogen peroxide and 1 teaspoon of clear ammonia and soak the stain for 10 minutes at a time, checking every 10 minutes and resoaking if necessary. Remember, fabrics need to be tested for color-fastness before using peroxide.

For dry-clean-only fabrics, flush the stain with club soda to prevent setting, then sponge the area with Energine Cleaning

Fluid®. If the stain persists, take it to your dry cleaner.

COFFEE AND TEA (black or with sugar): Blot up all that you can and, if the garment is washable, flush immediately with cold water. Rub detergent into the stain and work well between your thumbs before laundering as usual. If the stain is still visible and you can use hot water on the fabric, spread the stain over the sink, or stretch over a bowl and tie or rubber band in place (like a little trampoline), and set the bowl in the sink. Cover the stain with 20 Mule Team® Borax and pour boiling water through it, circling from the outside of the stain until you have reached the center. Let soak 30 minutes to an hour and relaunder.

For more delicate fabrics, soak in Brilliant Bleach™.

For sturdy whites, such as knits and T-shirts, dissolve 2 denture-cleaning tablets in warm water and soak the stain for 30 minutes. Check the garment. If the stain is still visible, soak again and launder as usual.

Out at a restaurant? Dip your napkin in

water and sprinkle with salt and blot the offending stain.

For stains from lattes and cappuccinos, see *Milk.*

COLA AND SOFT DRINKS: Sponge these spills as soon as possible with a solution of equal parts alcohol and water. On washable clothes, bleach out remaining stains with an equal mixture of 3 percent hydrogen peroxide and water. Saturate stain and wait 20 minutes. If the stain is gone, launder as usual. Repeat if the stain remains. You can also soak the fabric in a solution of Brilliant Bleach™ as directed on the container.

Borax is also effective in soft drink/cola removal. Moisten the spot thoroughly and sprinkle with borax, working well between your thumbs. Flush with water and re-treat if necessary.

Getting the stain out as soon as possible is important: cola and soft drinks will discolor fabrics as they oxidize.

COLLAR STAINS: This is for those women whose husbands won't share laundry duty, the women who didn't know that the wedding ring came with a ring around the collar! It's easy to remove, though. Just use some inexpensive shampoo! Shampoo dissolves body oils so it works great on that collar ring. Keep some in a bottle with a dispenser top in the laundry room. Squirt on enough to cover the offending stain and work it in well, then launder as usual.

COPIER TONER (powder): First, carefully shake off any loose powder and brush lightly with a soft brush. An old, soft toothbrush works well. Pretreat with your favorite spotter or try Zout® or Spot Shot Instant Carpet Stain Remover® and launder as usual, using the hottest water for the fabric type. Don't rub or brush with your hand. The oil in your skin will spread and set the stain.

COSMETICS (foundation, blusher, eye shadow, eyeliner, and mascara): Bar soap such as Dove®, Caress™ and other such beauty bars work well on cosmetics spots. Wet the stain and rub with the soap, working it in well. Flush with warm water and, once stain is removed, launder as usual.

Sometimes just working in laundry detergent will be all you need. For difficult cases, add some borax to the area and work well between your thumbs.

If your garment is dry-clean-only, try some Energine Cleaning Fluid® directly on the spot. Make sure to use a cool blow-dryer to keep a ring from forming on the fabric. You'll need to take the garment to a professional cleaner if the stain doesn't come out. (See also *Makeup*.)

CRAYON AND COLORED PENCIL: Place the stained area on a pad of paper towels and spray with WD-40 Lubricant®. Let stand for a few minutes, then turn the fabric over and spray the other side. Let sit for a further 10 minutes before working undiluted dishwashing liquid into the stained area to remove the crayon and oil. Replace the paper-toweling pad as necessary. Wash in the hottest possible water for the fabric, along with your normal detergent and appropriate bleaching agent (depending on whether the clothes are white or colored). Wash on the longest wash cycle available, and rinse well.

Another way to remove crayon from washable fabrics such as wool, acrylic, linen, cotton and polyester is to lay the offending stain between two pieces of brown paper and press with a warm/medium iron. A grocery bag works well—just remember to keep any ink that may be on the bag away from the fabric. The paper works as a blotter to absorb the crayon, so keep changing it as the wax is absorbed. If any color mark remains, soak the garment in Brilliant Bleach™ or flush with Energine Cleaning Fluid®.

Note: Don't panic if the crayon has also gone through the dryer. Simply spray an old rag with WD-40 Lubricant®; then thoroughly wipe down the drum. Make sure the dryer is empty when you do this—no clothes, no crayons. Place a load of dry rags in the dryer and run through a drying cycle when you're through. This will remove any oily residue.

DYE (see also *Hair Dye***):** Dye stains are difficult if not impossible to remove. Try one or all of these methods.

Spread the stained area over a bowl and put a rubber band around the fabric *and* the bowl to hold the fabric taut, like a trampoline. Set the bowl in the sink with the drain in the open position to allow the water to run freely away. Turn on the cold water faucet to a nice steady drip and let it drip through the dye spot for 3 to 6 hours. Monitor the sink to be sure the water is draining. This treatment is effective in many cases.

You can also try saturating the dye spot with a combination of equal parts 3 percent hydrogen peroxide and water. Set the fabric in the sun, keeping it moist with the solution until the spot completely disappears. Rinse well and launder as usual. Use only on color-fast clothes.

If your dye problem is caused from fugitive color—that is, color that has run from one fabric to another during the wash cycle—all the bleaching in the world won't help. Try Synthrapol™ or Carbona Color Run Remover™ instead.

Quilters have used Synthrapol™ for years to remove color that runs in homemade quilts.

Make sure to read *all* the directions on the bottle prior to using.

Carbona Color Run Remover™ is extremely effective on cotton fabrics. It is not for delicates or some blends, so do read the box with care. It may also cause damage to buttons and, in some cases, zippers. You may want to remove these prior to treating.

EGG: First scrape off any solid matter. Then, soak the fabric in a glass or plastic container with any enzyme-soaking product, such as Biz Non Chlorine Bleach™. Soak for at least 6 hours or overnight. If a stain remains, work in powder detergent, rubbing vigorously between your thumbs. Rinse and wash as usual. Check the garment carefully for any remaining stain when you remove it from the washer. Don't apply heat until all of the stain is removed or the stain will become permanent.

You can also try treating the area with cool water and unseasoned meat tenderizer. Work this into the area well, and allow it to sit for a few hours, being sure to keep the area moist. Continue treating until no stain remains.

Take nonwashables to the dry cleaner as soon as possible. Quick treatment is important. Make sure you identify the stain to your cleaner so it can be treated properly and promptly.

EYELINER AND EYE SHADOW: See *Cosmetics.*

FABRIC SOFTENER SPOTS: For the greasy spots that sometimes appear on clothes after drying with dryer fabric softener sheets, dampen the spot and rub with pure bar soap and relaunder.

For spots from liquid fabric softener, rub with undiluted liquid dish soap and relaunder.

FELT TIP MARKER: See *Marker.*

FOOD DYE: Fruit juices, gelatin desserts, fruit smoothies, and frozen fruit sticks all contain food dye that can leave a nasty stain on clothes.

Treating the stain while it is still fresh is the very best thing you can do. If you are out in public and don't have access to any cleaning supplies, wet the spot with club soda or cool water and blot, blot, blot. If you are at home, then treat the spot with 1 cup of cool water to which you have added 1 tablespoon of ammonia. Once you have flushed the spot well with this solution, grab the salt shaker and rub salt into the wound . . . I mean stain! Let this sit for an hour or so, and then brush off the salt. If the stain is still visible, re-treat the same way.

You can also try stretching the fabric tight and holding it under a forceful stream of cold water. This will flush out much of the spot without spreading it. Next, rub in your favorite detergent, scrubbing vigorously between your thumbs. Rinse again in cool water. Do not apply heat to the stain until it is completely removed.

I have had great success soaking food dye spills in Brilliant Bleach™ (follow the directions for hand-soaking on the container).

If you are dealing with a red, orange, or purple stain, try Wine Away Red Wine Stain Remover™, used according to directions. Don't be fooled by the name—it is great for all red-type stains. You will be amazed!

Remember, if the stain is not removed during the spotting process, it will not come out in the laundry!

FRUIT AND FRUIT JUICE (also see *Berries*): These stains absolutely must be removed before the fabric is washed. The combination of heat and age will set fruit stains and they will be impossible to remove, even for the Queen.

Sponge or spray the area immediately with soda water or seltzer. If these products aren't available, use cold water. *Do not use hot water.* Rinse the offending spot as soon as possible while it is still wet. Rub in your favorite detergent and scrub the area between your thumbs. *Now* rinse under hot running water—as hot as the fabric can tolerate. Pull the fabric taut and allow the full force of the water to flow through the area. The stronger the flow the better.

If the stain is still visible after this treatment, make a paste of 20 Mule Team® Borax and warm water, and work it into the stained area. Let this dry and brush off. Repeat as needed. You can also try pulling the fabric tight over a bowl, using a rubber band to secure it. Sprinkle 20 Mule Team® Borax over the stain and, using the hottest water possible for the fabric type, start at the outside edge of the stain and pour the water through the borax in circles until you are pouring through the center of the stain.

Fresh fruit stains, if treated promptly, will usually come out. Quick treatment is especially important for fruits such as peach and citrus.

Old Fruit Stains: Before you can remove the stain you must reconstitute it. You can do this by applying glycerin to the area. Rub it in well and allow to soak for 30 minutes. Treat as above.

For nonwashable fabrics, gently sponge the stain with cold water as soon as it occurs and then take to a dry cleaner as quickly as possible. Be sure to identify the stain so it can be treated properly.

If the stains are red in nature, use Wine Away Red Wine Stain Remover™ as directed in the section on berry stains.

FURNITURE POLISH: Furniture polish is usually an oil-based stain, so it must be reconstituted. Restore the oil in the polish by spraying with WD-40 Lubricant®. Allow the lubricant to soak for 10 minutes, then work in undiluted dishwashing liquid. Work this in well between your thumbs to remove the grease. Flush with a forceful stream of the hottest water you can for the fabric type. Pretreat with a product such as Zout®, which is great for grease spots, and launder as usual.

You can also try cleaning the area with Energine Cleaning Fluid®, used according to can directions.

If the furniture polish has color in it, refer to the section on dye.

GLUE, ADHESIVES, MUCILAGE: Modern adhesives and glues are very hard to remove. You may have to use a special solvent. Take the garment to the dry cleaner and be sure to identify the spot.

Here's a rundown of glue types and how to remove them.

Model Glue: Can usually be removed with nail polish remover containing acetone, although you may need to purchase straight acetone at the hardware store or the beauty supply. Always test the acetone in a small area first.

Plastic Adhesives: For best results, treat these stains before they dry. Try washing in cool water and detergent. If the stain remains, bring 1 cup or so of white vinegar to a boil, and immerse the stain. Have more vinegar boiling as you treat the stain so that you can switch to the hot vinegar as soon as the first cup starts to cool. Continue reheating the vinegar and treating for 15 to 20 minutes.

Rubber Cement: Scrape off all that you can with a dull, straight edge that you can throw away. (Don't use a credit card for this—unless it's over its limit!) Treat with Energine Cleaning Fluid® as directed.

You can also try working petroleum jelly into the glue until it pills into balls that you can then scrape from the fabric. Treat the area with undiluted liquid dish soap and launder in the hottest water the fabric will tolerate.

Miscellaneous Glues: Sponge or rinse the fabric in warm water. Work in your favorite powdered detergent or liquid detergent along with some 20 Mule Team® Borax. Rub vigorously between your thumbs. Rinse and wash in the hottest water you can for the fabric type.

Remember, soap and water will remove most synthetic glue when the spot is fresh. Acetone will remove most clear, plastic cement-type glues. Make sure to test acetone in an inconspicuous area, and never use on acetate fabrics—it will dissolve them.

For old, dried glue stains, soak the fabric in a solution of boiling hot white vinegar and water. Use 2 parts white vinegar to every 10 parts of water and soak for 30 to 60 minutes. You may need to scrape off the glue as it softens. Then pretreat and launder as usual.

GRASS, FLOWERS AND FOLIAGE: There are several ways to remove grass stains from fabrics. Pick one and try it. If it doesn't completely remove the stain, try another. Don't put clothes into the dryer until the grass stain is removed.

First a word of caution: Avoid using alkalis such as ammonia, degreasers or alkaline detergents. They interact with the tannin in the grass stains and may permanently set the stain.

Okay—first, washable fabrics: Sponge on rubbing alcohol, repeating several times. If the stain persists, sponge with white vinegar and rinse. Work in your favorite laundry detergent and rinse well.

Rubbing white nongel toothpaste into grass stains will often remove them. Rub well, then rinse and wash as usual.

For jeans, apply undiluted alcohol to the area and allow to soak 15 minutes before laundering as usual.

Zout® and Spot Shot Carpet Stain Remover® also work very well on grass stains. Follow the label directions. Biz All Fabric Bleach™ made into a paste with cold water is effective in treating stubborn grass stains too.

For grass on white leather shoes, rub the grass stain with molasses and leave it on the shoe overnight. Wash the molasses off with hot soap and water, and the grass stain should be gone.

For grass on suede fabric, including shoes, rub the stain with a sponge dipped in glycerin. Then rub with a cloth dipped in undiluted white vinegar, brush the nap gently to reset, and allow to dry and brush again. Remember: test in an inconspicuous spot first.

GRAVY: With gravy you need to remove the starch used to thicken it, so you will want to soak the garment in cold water long enough to dissolve the starch. It may take several hours.

Pretreat prior to laundering with a good spotter, such as Zout®, Spot Shot Carpet Stain Remover® or Whink Wash Away Laundry Stain Remover™. Launder in the hottest possible water for the fabric type.

You can also soak the garment in Brilliant Bleach™, for days if necessary.

GREASE AND OIL (including cooking oil and salad dressing): Grease and oil must be removed thoroughly, otherwise a semitransparent stain will set and will turn dark from all the soil it attracts.

To treat a grease stain it helps to know whether it is from animal oil, vegetable oil or automotive oil.

To remove a grease stain, first remove as much of the greasy substance as possible without forcing the grease farther down into the fabric fibers. Use a paper towel to blot and absorb all the grease that you can. Next, apply a drawing agent such as baking soda, cornstarch, or talcum powder. Rub it in gently and let it sit for 15 to 30 minutes to allow the agent to absorb and draw the grease out of the fabric. Brush the powder off thoroughly and check the stain. If it looks like you can absorb more grease, repeat the process.

Next, lay the fabric over a thick rag or a heavy fold of paper towels. Working from the back of the fabric, blot with Energine Cleaning Fluid®. Change the pad under the fabric as needed and repeat if necessary.

When grease stains are stubborn, we need to fall back on the idea that grease removes grease. Spray the grease spot with WD-40 Lubricant® and let it soak for 10 minutes, then work in undiluted dishwashing liquid and work well between your thumbs. Flush with the hottest water you can for the fabric, pre-treat and launder as usual. Do not use this method on silk or crease-resistant finishes.

Many grease stains will eventually turn yellow when set with age and heat. Treat these stains by soaking in diluted hydrogen peroxide or Brilliant Bleach™. Don't use this process unless you know that the clothes are colorfast.

Use Energine Cleaning Fluid® on dry-clean-only fabrics, or take to a professional dry cleaner.

For heavily soiled, greasy work clothes, try pouring a can of original Coca-Cola® in the washer with your detergent and launder as usual. The combination of sugar and cola syrup works wonders!

GUM: The best way to deal with gum is to harden it first. Harden any item marred by chewing gum by placing it in a plastic bag in the freezer and leaving it overnight. Immediately upon removing the bag from the freezer, scrape off any gum that you can with a dull straight edge. If all the gum is removed, treat the fabric with an equal mixture of white vinegar and liquid dish soap. You may also try treating the area with lighter fluid, although you must do this outside and use extreme care, testing the fabric first.

Sometimes rubbing the area with egg white

(*not* the yolk—no joke!) will remove the remaining residue.

If gum is still trapped, try working petroleum jelly into the fibers, and scraping off the little balls that form. Be sure to follow the directions under **Grease** in this section to remove the grease from the petroleum jelly.

Petroleum jelly will also soften old, dry gum. You want to work the petroleum jelly into the gum and then scrape off all that you can.

For those of you who ask, yes, peanut butter will work too, but it is messier. My advice is to eat the peanut butter and use the petroleum jelly!

Carbona® makes a Stain Devil for Chewing Gum Removal. It's a great little specialty spotter.

For dry-clean-only fabrics, you may freeze the fabric and scrape off what gum you can. Take it to your dry cleaner right away.

HAIR DYE: If you didn't listen to me when I told you to dye your hair naked in the backyard, then hair-dye spots may be a major problem for you. Here's what to do:

Clothing or fabrics stained with hair dye should be washed in warm water, to which you have added white vinegar and your normal detergent. Do this in a sink or container, adding about 2 tablespoons of detergent and 2 cups of white vinegar to a gallon of warm water. Let it soak for several hours.

If the stain still remains, try our favorite bleach, Brilliant Bleach™. You can soak whites and colorfast fabrics for several days if necessary, without damage. Try to avoid the hair-dye problem if you can. I suggest using the same old towel when you do your hair.

HAND CREAM: Blot off all that you can and treat with Energine Cleaning Fluid®, working from the back of the fabric. Once all of the stain is removed, launder as usual.

ICE CREAM: Yummy-yummy in the tummy—not so great on clothes! Sponge the garment as quickly as possible with cold water, club soda, or seltzer. If a stain still remains, treat it with cold water and unseasoned meat tenderizer. Let this soak on the fabric for about 30 minutes or so and then flush with cold water to see if the offending spot is gone. Pretreat with Spot Shot Carpet Stain Remover® or Zout® and launder as usual.

If a grease spot remains, treat with Energine Cleaning Fluid® working from the back of the fabric over a pad of paper towels to absorb the spot and the spotting solution.

Sometimes treating ice cream–stained fabric with a small amount of ammonia will also work. Then, of course, launder as usual.

INK: How can one little pen cause so much grief? The first line of offense is rubbing alcohol. Sponge the ink mark, or dip it into a glass of rubbing alcohol, letting it soak until the offending spot is removed. Don't be tricked into using hair spray. That may have worked in the past, but hair spray now contains a lot of oil, and that just spreads the stain.

Denatured alcohol—a much stronger version of rubbing alcohol—may be more effective. Test this first in an inconspicuous spot, as denatured alcohol may damage some fabrics.

You also can try using acetone. This too

must be tested. (And remember, *never* use acetone on acetates.)

White, nongel toothpaste rubbed firmly and vigorously into the stain may work. After this method be sure to pretreat and launder as usual.

Often just soaking ink stains in milk will dissolve them.

Turpentine is effective on very challenging ink stains. Working over a pad of paper towels, tap the spot on the back of the fabric using the back of a spoon or an old toothbrush. Don't rub. Work in undiluted dishwashing liquid prior to laundering, and wash in the hottest water possible for the fabric type. Dispose of all paper, etc., saturated with turpentine immediately—outside, please.

Some inks only respond to solvents, so you may need to use Energine Cleaning Fluid®.

On leather, remove ballpoint ink by rubbing with cuticle remover or petroleum jelly. You may need to leave it on the stained area for several days to achieve success.

On vinyl, believe it or not, the best thing is for you to be so mad that you could spit!

Saliva will remove ballpoint ink from vinyl—as long as you are quick. Apply generously and wipe with a soft cloth. For old stains, apply glycerin, let it soak for 30 minutes or so, and then attempt to wash the stain away with a wet soft cloth rubbed over a bar of soap.

KETCHUP: See *Tomato-Based Stains*.

KOOL-AID™: Flush the spot as quickly as possible with club soda and then hold under forceful running water. If a stained area still remains, soak in Brilliant Bleach™ until the stain is removed. This may take hours or days, depending on the fabric and the stain. Soak only white or colorfast clothes in Brilliant Bleach™.

For red, grape, fruit punch, and other red Kool-Aid™ flavors, treat with Wine Away Red Wine Stain Remover™ for instantaneous stain removal.

LIPSTICK: Lipstick is actually an oily dye stain. Water, heat or wet spotters will only spread it and make the problem worse and set the stain.

Rub in vegetable oil, WD-40 Lubricant® or

mineral oil and let it sit on the spot for 15 to 30 minutes. Next sponge the area with a little ammonia—sudsy or clear is fine.

Now, before you launder, work in undiluted liquid dish soap to be sure you have removed all of the oil.

Another method I have had real success with is GOJO Crème Waterless Hand Cleaner™. Look for this at hardware stores and home centers. Work it into the lipstick, rubbing between your thumbs vigorously. Launder as usual. This method is great for the smear of lipstick on cloth table napkins.

In an emergency, try spraying the spot with a little hair spray. Let this sit for a few minutes and then wipe gently with a damp cloth. Test this method in an inconspicuous spot first.

You will also find that Zout®, Spot Shot Carpet Stain Remover® and Whink Wash Away Laundry Spotter™ are generally effective on lipstick.

For really stubborn, old stains, try moistening with denatured alcohol, then treat with undiluted liquid dish soap.

If you are getting dressed and you accidentally get lipstick on your clothes, try rubbing the stain with white bread. (Yes, it has to be white!)

MAKEUP (oily foundation, powder, cream blush, cover creams): Sprinkle baking soda on the makeup smudge, then brush the area with an old wet toothbrush until the makeup is removed. Nongel white toothpaste scrubbed with a toothbrush is also effective.

Liquid dish soap or shampoo will generally remove makeup stains. Work the product into the stain vigorously between your thumbs.

For stubborn makeup stains use nonoily makeup remover, pretreat and launder as usual. (See also *Cosmetics*.)

MARKER, WASHABLE: Rinse the stain from the fabric with cold water until no more color can be removed. Place the fabric on paper towels and saturate the back of the fabric with alcohol, using a cotton ball to blot the stain. Replace the paper towels as needed as they absorb the color. Work in Fels-Naptha Soap® until the spot is well lathered and wash in hot water with laundry detergent and fabric appropriate bleach. Rinse in warm water.

MARKER, PERMANENT: First of all, permanent usually means permanent. But before you give up and throw in the towel—or blouse, or pants, or whatever—here are some things to try.

Fill a glass with denatured alcohol (use a size appropriate to the stain) and dip the stained area into the alcohol, allowing it to soak. If it appears that the marker is being removed, continue the process.

If the stain appears stubborn, try scrubbing the marker spot with an old toothbrush, white, nongel toothpaste, and some baking soda. Give it a really good scrubbing. Rinse. If the marker stain is almost gone, soak in a cup of warm water and 2 denture-cleaning tablets for whites, and Brilliant Bleach™ for colorfast clothes. This will require some time, but the stain all comes out, so it's worth it.

If the marker is still there, scrub with Lava™ soap prior to trying the denture-cleaning tablets or bleach.

Good luck. And look out for those big black permanent markers and those Sharpies™. They're great pens, but they're murder on clothes! I can't even tell you how many times I have "accidentally" written on my clothes during a book signing with a Sharpie™ in my hand!

MAYONNAISE: See *Grease.*

MEAT JUICES: Once dry, meat juices are very tough to remove, so it's important to react quickly. Sponge the area immediately with cold water (not hot—it will set the stain), or with club soda. Next, apply unseasoned meat tenderizer and cold water, working the mixture in well. Let it sit for 30 to 60 minutes. Pretreat and launder as usual, but be sure to use *cool* water.

On dry-clean-only fabrics, sponge with cold water and take to a professional cleaner.

MEDICINES: It would be impossible to list all the medicines on the market. But this section should give you an idea of what to look out for, as well as what to do for each family of medicine.

Alcohol: Medicines containing alcohol stain quickly. Treat these stains as you would spilled alcohol.

Iron: Iron or medicines containing iron products should be treated as rust.

Oily Medicines: Oily medicines should be treated with a degreasing product. I have had great luck with Soapworks At Home All-Purpose Cleaner™, used undiluted. Work it in well and then rinse.

You can also treat these stains as you would an oil or grease stain.

Syrups: Cough syrup or children's medicines can usually be removed with water. Soak the fabric with cool water as soon as possible. Running cold water full force through the fabric can be helpful, and you may also want to try working in Fels-Naptha®, or soaking the stain in Biz Non Chlorine Bleach™ or Brilliant Bleach™. If the syrup is red, use Wine Away Red Wine Stain Remover™. (See, I told you not to be fooled by its name! It is murder on red stains!)

MILDEW: Mildew is a fungus that grows and

flourishes in warm, humid, dark conditions, like the shower, the basement, etc. The best way to avoid mildew is to ensure that things are totally dry *before* you put them away. Invisible spores can quickly grow to huge proportions, especially on natural materials such as cotton, wool, leather, paper, wood, etc.

Air needs to circulate to keep mildew from forming, so do not crowd clothes into closets.

Store clothing only after it has been cleaned and dried thoroughly.

If you are storing things such as leather purses, belts, shoes, even suitcases, clean them well, then set them in the sun for an hour or so. Do not store things in plastic as this caters to damp conditions.

If you smell a damp or musty smell coming from a closet, suspect mildew immediately and act quickly to dry it out. Even allowing a fan to blow in the closet overnight can make a huge difference by drying and circulating the air.

Okay—here's what to do if you already have mildew stains on fabrics. First, try working some Fels-Naptha Laundry Bar Soap® into the area and laundering. If stains remain and the fabric will tolerate chlorine bleach, soak it in 1 gallon of cold water to which you have added 2 to 3 tablespoons of chlorine bleach.

Moistening white or colorfast clothes with lemon juice, sprinkling them with salt and laying the garment in the sun may also remove mildew. If in doubt, test this method first.

Leather presents a different challenge. Take the item outside and brush off all the powdery mildew that you can with a soft brush. Wipe the leather with equal parts of rubbing alcohol and water, or try massaging cuticle remover into the area. After 10 minutes, wipe vigorously with a soft cloth.

Wash leather with a complexion bar soap such as Dove® or Caress™ and buff dry—do not rinse.

Remember: with mildew, the best defense is a good offense, so try to keep it from occurring.

MILK/CREAM/WHIPPING CREAM/HALF AND HALF: Rinse fabric under a cold, forceful stream of water from the faucet. Treat with unseasoned meat tenderizer and cool water. Allow to soak for 30 minutes; then flush with cool water again. If greasy-looking marks remain, treat with Energine Cleaning Fluid®, working from the back of the fabric over a heavy pad of paper towels. Launder as usual.

Treat washable fabrics stained from milk by flushing with cool water before working in detergent and a little ammonia. Wash in cool water and air-dry.

For dry-clean-only fabrics, take to a professional as soon as possible and identify the stain when you drop off the item.

MUD: The key word here is *dry.* Let mud dry. Never treat a wet mud stain other than lifting off any solid pieces with a dull straight edge. Once mud has dried, take the vacuum cleaner and vacuum the area with the hose attachment. You'll achieve the greatest suction that way. This may be a two-person job: one to hold the fabric, one to hold the hose.

Rub the cut side of a potato over the mud stain and launder as usual.

For stubborn stains, sponge with equal portions of rubbing alcohol and cool water. For red mud stains, treat with a rust remover (see *Rust*). Rubbing 20 Mule Team® Borax into a dampened mud stain will often remove it.

Spraying with Spot Shot Carpet Stain Remover® prior to laundering is also helpful.

MUSTARD: The word makes me shiver! This is a terrible stain to attempt (notice I said *attempt*) to remove.

The turmeric in mustard is what gives mustard its distinctive bright yellow color—it's also what would make it a darn good dye!

Remove as much of the mustard as possible, using a dull straight edge. Next, flex the fabric to break the grip of the embedded residue on the fabric fibers. Apply glycerin (hand cream section, drugstore) and let it sit at least an hour. Pretreat and launder as usual.

If the fabric is white or colorfast, soak the stain in hydrogen peroxide for 30 minutes. Again, Brilliant Bleach™ may remove the stain after a lengthy soaking.

For white clothes, dissolve a denture-cleaning tablet in ½ cup of cool water and allow the stained area to soak.

Things to avoid: Ammonia and heat. They will both set the stain and you will never get it out.

Kind of makes you think that ketchup and relish are all you need on that hotdog, doesn't it!

MYSTERY STAINS: These are spots and spills that you have no idea where they came from. The unknowns. Here's what to do:

• Blot with cool water (hot water sets stains).

• Blot with a sponge or cloth dampened with water and a teaspoon or so of white vinegar (not for cotton or linen).

• Blot with a sponge or cloth dampened with water and a teaspoon or so of clear ammonia (again, not for cotton or linen).

• Blot with rubbing alcohol diluted 50/50 with cool water.

• Sponge with a solution of Brilliant Bleach™ and water.

NAIL POLISH: Okay, if you had polished your nails naked in the backyard you wouldn't be reading this, would you? Stretch the fabric over a glass bowl and make a little trampoline by securing the fabric with a rubber band. Drip acetone-based polish remover through the stain with a stainless steel spoon (not silver) and tap the stain with the edge of the spoon. Continue dripping the acetone through the fabric until the polish is removed. This requires time and patience. If you run out of either, walk away and come back later. Straight acetone, purchased at the hardware store or beauty supply, may work faster, but be sure to test an area first.

If a color stain remains after the polish is removed, dilute hydrogen peroxide (50 percent peroxide, 50 percent water), apply to the stain, and set the fabric in the sun, keeping it moist with the peroxide solution. Do this only for white or colorfast clothes.

Do not use acetone on silk or acetates, and always test the acetone on an inconspicuous area prior to beginning.

Nonwashable fabrics should be dry-cleaned.

ODORS: Eliminate odors, don't use a perfumed cover-up. I like ODORZOUT™ odor eliminator because it absorbs odors and removes them permanently—without leaving any telltale smells behind. It is nontoxic and safe for all surfaces, and it can be used wet or dry. It is also safe for the environment and a little goes a long way. Keep some on hand. It's great for just about any odor you're likely to come across, such as smoke, mildew, mold, feces, urine, food odors, any kind of odor. Do not use a perfumed cover-up.

OIL *(also see Grease and Oil):* Blot up all oil quickly. Avoid rubbing or you will force the oil farther into the fibers. Pretreat washable fabrics with your favorite spot remover, or use one recommended for oily stains in this book. Launder in the hottest possible water for the fabric.

Nonwashables should be dry-cleaned.

OINTMENT (A and D ointment, Desitin, zinc oxide): Anyone who has had a baby will be familiar with this problem stain. Use hot water and detergent, rubbing the fabric against itself to remove the oil. If the stain remains, treat as indicated in the section on *Grease and Oil*.

For zinc oxide, soak the garment in white vinegar for 30 minutes after treating as above, then launder as usual.

PAINT, LATEX: Treat this stain immediately for best results. It is important to remove paint *before* it dries, so keep the stain wet if you can't work on it right away.

Flush the paint from the fabric with a forceful stream of warm water. Next, treat the stain with a solution of liquid dish soap and water, or laundry detergent and water. Work it into the stained area, soaping and rinsing until the stain is removed. Do this as many times as necessary. If the fabric is color-fast, you can also work in some automatic dishwasher detergent and let it soak on the fabric for 5 to 10 minutes before laundering as usual.

You can also try a product aptly named

OOPS!™ Just follow the directions on the can closely.

On fabrics such as cotton and polyester, try spraying the garment with oven cleaner and letting it sit about 15 to 30 minutes before flushing with plenty of water. Use *extreme* care with this method and use it at your own risk. Some fabrics cannot tolerate the oven cleaner, but if the garment is ruined by the paint, it is worth a try. Also use care where you spray the oven cleaner and what you set the fabric on afterward.

PAINT, OIL-BASED: Get busy and remove this spill ASAP. You're out of luck if it dries. If you must go to the store for products, keep the spill moist: *Do not allow oil-based paint to dry.*

Check the paint can and use the thinner recommended by the manufacturer. Sometimes thinner for correction fluid will also work. Remember to test an area first with these two methods.

I fall back on turpentine when all else fails. Work the turpentine into the spill, and once the paint is removed, work in GOJO Crème Waterless Hand Cleaner™. That will take out the oiliness from the turpentine. Remember to dispose of turpentine soaked rags or paper towels outside, as soon as possible.

When working on a paint spill, work from the back of the fabric over a thick pad of paper towels. Tap the stained area with an old toothbrush or an old spoon as you work to force the paint out.

Now that you have removed the stain, saturate it with detergent and work in vigorously. Cover the area with the hottest water you can use for the fabric, and let it soak overnight. Scrub again, between your thumbs, and launder as usual.

PENCIL: Okay, how easy is this? Take a nice, clean, soft eraser, and gently rub the offending mark away! Just be sure the eraser is clean, or you will create a large stain. If the spot is stubborn, sponge with Energine Cleaning Fluid®.

PERFUME: Follow the directions in the section on *Alcoholic Beverages.* A few words to the wise: The best time to put it on is right before you put on your clothes, not after. And never spray perfume directly on your clothes. This will damage them. The combination of alcohol and oil is death to fabrics.

PERSPIRATION STAINS: These stains are really the pits. Perspiration will weaken fabrics, so treat vulnerable areas with care and treat those invisible perspiration problems right after you wear a garment for the first time—*before* you toss it in the washer.

Moisten the underarm area—or any other spot where perspiration stains are a problem—and work in a lather of Fels-Naptha Soap®. Once you've worked up a good lather, toss the garment in the machine and launder as usual.

Working Biz Activated Non Chlorine Bleach™ into the stained fabric is also effective. Just make sure to wet the offending area first!

Always treat perspiration areas on a garment *prior* to laundering. If odor is present, apply warm water to the area and work in 20 Mule Team® Borax. Let sit 30 minutes or so, then launder.

If you already have stains, try dampening the fabric with warm water and working in laundry detergent and Biz™. Let that soak about 30 minutes and launder as usual.

I have found that soaking garments (whites or colors) in Brilliant Bleach™ from Soapworks® is very effective for removing underarm stains.

You can also try to clean existing stains with heated white vinegar. Spray it on the fabric and then work in 20 Mule Team® Borax. This works well on odor as well as stains.

If the fabric has changed color, try spraying with sudsy ammonia, let sit about 15 minutes, then launder as usual.

Bear in mind that yellowed or discolored fabric may be damaged. The garment may not be salvageable.

Treat everything prior to washing for the first time and do try switching brands of antiperspirant. Never wear shirts or blouses more than one day if you have a perspiration problem. You may find that wearing natural fibers such as cottons will be less of a problem than polyester and polyester blends. If your problem is serious you may want to try underarm shields. They trap moisture before it can reach the fabric. They can be removed and thrown away each day, and can't be seen through the garment. Look for them in lingerie stores and in catalogs. Also check out the section in this stain removal guide on *Antiperspirants and Deodorants.*

PURPLE OR BLUISH COLOR ON SYNTHETIC FIBERS: Sometimes synthetic fibers will develop a purple tinge after repeated laundering. Remove it with Rit Color Remover™ and launder as usual.

RUST: On white fabrics, saturate with lemon juice and sprinkle with salt, then lay in the sun. (No, not you—the fabric!) If the rust is stubborn, apply the lemon juice and salt, and pour water through the stain. Use boiling water if the fabric will tolerate it; otherwise use hot. Check the care label.

You can also cover the stained area with cream of tartar, then gather up the edges of the fabric and dip the spot in hot water. Let stand 5 to 10 minutes and then launder as usual.

There are good commercial rust removers on the market. Try Whink Rust Remover®, Magica®, and Rust Magic®. Be sure to read directions carefully when using commercial rust removers. Some cannot be used on colored fabric, so check carefully.

SAP, PINE TAR: See *Tar.*

SCORCH MARKS: Sorry to say, but severe scorch marks cannot be removed.

Light scorch marks may be treated with a cloth dampened with 1 part 3 percent hydrogen peroxide and 3 parts water. Lay the cloth over the scorch mark and press with a medium/hot iron. Do not iron off of the cloth or you will scorch the fabric again. Make sure to try this method first in a small, inconspicuous space.

If the scorch is still visible, moisten the spot with the diluted peroxide and lay it in the sun.

Very light scorch marks may also be removed by wetting them with water and laying the garment in the sun.

If the scorch mark has appeared on white clothes, saturate the scorched area with lemon juice and lay it in the sun. Keep it moist with the lemon juice until the stain is removed.

For white cottons, sometimes boiling in ½ cup of soap and 2 quarts of milk will remove the stain. Try this at your own risk. Some fabrics may not tolerate boiling.

For light scorches you can also rub the fabric with the cut side of a white onion (not a red onion—it will stain) and then soak the fabric in cold water for several hours. Launder as usual.

Remember: scorching weakens fibers, so use care and always relaunder the item once the scorch mark has been removed.

SHOE POLISH: Work laundry detergent into the fabric immediately and rinse. For persistent stains, sponge with alcohol. Use undiluted alcohol on white clothes, and 1 part alcohol to 2 parts water on colored fabrics. Rinse again, or try using turpentine after first testing in an inconspicuous spot.

Shoe polish has an oily base containing dye. Using the wrong things such as water, heat, or wet spotters will spread and set the stain.

Work in vegetable oil or WD-40 Lubricant® and let it sit for 15 minutes. Sponge on a little ammonia (not on silk, please), then work in undiluted dishwashing liquid and launder as usual.

Energine Cleaning Fluid® may also help to eliminate the final stained area.

If you have any discoloration remaining from the dye in the shoe polish, soak the fabric in Brilliant Bleach™ until the stain is removed.

If the shoe polish stain is old and heavy, you may need to treat it with petroleum jelly. Cover the polish and work in the petroleum jelly, let it soak for 30 to 60 minutes, and then scrape off all that you can of the polish and the petroleum jelly. Work in undiluted dishwashing liquid and flush with a forceful stream of hot water. Pretreat and launder as usual.

Liquid Shoe Polish: Blot up all that you can from the fabric. Do not rub—this will spread the stain. Do not apply water. Instead, saturate with alcohol—undiluted for whites, diluted as above for colors. Continue to flush with alcohol, work in your favorite laundry detergent, and then rub vigorously to remove all trace of the stain.

SILK SPOTS: Spots on silk are hard to remove and must be handled with care.

Dry-cleaning solvent may spot-clean silk, but you're likely to be left with a ring on the fabric. Make sure to use the blow-dryer on the spot to avoid that telltale ring.

For unusual or heavy stains, take to a professional. Too much rubbing can remove the color from silk.

SILLY PUTTY®: First of all, let gravity do the work for you. Lay the fabric over a bowl and let the Silly Putty® simply drop off. You'll only have to clean up what's left!

Scrape off the balance of any Silly Putty® with a dull edge, such as an old credit card or knife back. Spray with WD-40 Lubricant® and let stand a few minutes. Scrape again, removing all the Silly Putty® that you can. Continue to do this, changing from the dull straight edge to cotton balls. If any stain remains, saturate a cotton ball with rubbing alcohol, blot the stain, and rinse. Work in liquid dish soap and launder as usual in the hottest water you can for the fabric type.

If you don't have WD-40 Lubricant®, use petroleum jelly instead.

SOFT DRINKS: See *Cola and Soft Drinks.*

SOOT: Launder clothing in the hottest possible water for the fabric with your normal detergent, ½ cup of 20 Mule Team® Borax and ½ cup of Arm and Hammer Washing Soda™.

STICKERS: Heat white vinegar and apply it, undiluted, directly to the fabric. Allow the vinegar to soak until the sticker can be peeled back with ease.

TAR: Lift off as much solid matter as possible using a plastic (disposable) knife. Spread the stained area over a heavy pad of paper towels and apply glycerin to the fabric, tapping it with the back of an old toothbrush or plastic spoon. Change the paper towels as they absorb the tar. Finally, once you have removed all the tar you can, work in some turpentine or eucalyptus oil. Flush the stained area with alcohol, or work in undiluted liquid dish soap. Pretreat and launder as usual. Spot Shot Carpet Stain Remover® is a good spotter for this.

Dried Tar: Warm the glycerin or some olive oil and spread over the area, allowing it to soak until the tar is loosened. Then proceed as above.

Nonwashables should be taken to the dry cleaner as soon as possible.

TEA: See *Coffee and Tea.*

TOMATO-BASED STAINS (ketchup, spaghetti sauce, tomato sauce, barbecue sauce, etc.): Flush these stains well with cool water as soon as possible. Make sure you apply water to the back of the fabric. Apply white vinegar and then flush again with a forceful stream of water.

Apply Wine Away Red Wine Stain Remover™ per package directions.

URINE: Fresh urine stains are fairly easy to remove. First rinse well, flushing with lots of cool water. Presoak using an enzyme powder or Biz All Fabric Bleach™. Then launder as usual.

You may also soak urine-stained fabric in salt water, then rinse and launder as usual.

If the color of the fabric has changed due to the urine, sponge the area or spray with clear ammonia, then rinse and launder as usual.

For Old Urine Stains: Soak in clear hot water for an hour—the hotter the better. Add detergent and wash as usual, then rinse. Use the appropriate bleach for the fabric type, or Brilliant Bleach™ if you prefer.

See also the treatment mentioned under **Odors.**

VOMIT: Shake off or scrape what you can over the toilet. Flush the fabric from the "wrong" side with cool water, using a forceful stream. Once you have removed solid matter and excess liquid, make a paste of liquid laundry soap and 20 Mule Team® Borax and vigorously scrub the fabric. Rinse with salt water, pretreat and launder as usual.

Quick treatment is important to avoid stains from foods and stomach acid.

See also the treatment mentioned for **Odors**.

WINE: Never serve red wine without having white wine; nearby! And always tend to the stain *as soon as you can!*

For red wine spills, dilute the spot with white wine; then flush with cool water and apply salt.

If no white wine is available, sprinkle heavily with salt and flush with club soda or cool water.

Applying a paste of 20 Mule Team® Borax and water usually works.

For red wine spills and other red stains, keep Wine Away Red Wine Stain Remover™ on hand. It is totally nontoxic and works so fast on red wine and red stains that even I am still amazed. The directions are simple and easy. Blot up the spill, apply the Wine Away™, and watch the red stain disappear. Blot with a wet cloth. You'll thank me many times for this one!

YELLOW SPOTS AND STAINS: These stains are common on white clothes and linens. Denture-cleaning tablets will generally remove these stains. Fill a basin with water and add 1 or 2 tablets. Allow the tablets to dissolve and then soak the fabric until the yellow is removed.

RESOURCE GUIDE

ACETONE: A great spotter, but be careful. It is exceedingly strong and can damage fibers. Look for this at hardware stores, home centers and beauty supply stores.

ACT NATURAL CLOTHS®: See Euronet USA.

BIZ® ACTIVATED NON CHLORINE BLEACH: A great all-purpose powdered bleach. Look for it in the laundry aisle at grocery stores and discount stores.

BORAX: Better known as 20 Mule Team® Borax Laundry Additive. This can be found in the detergent aisle.

BRILLIANT BLEACH™: See Soapworks®.

CARBONA® COLOR RUN REMOVER: Removes fugitive color from fabrics. Available in grocery and discount stores.

CARBONA® STAIN DEVILS: A great series of spotters that target specific stains, like gum, blood, milk, etc.

CLEAR AMMONIA: There are two types of ammonia, clear and sudsy (sometimes called "cloudy"). Clear doesn't contain soap and should be used where suggested for that reason.

CLEAN SHIELD® SURFACE TREATMENT (formerly Invisible Shield®): This is such a wonderful product—just the name gives me goose bumps! It turns all of those hard-to-clean surfaces in your home (the exterior of the washing machine and dryer, any surface that is not wood or painted) into nonstick surfaces that can be cleaned with water and a soft cloth. No more soap scum or hard-water deposits! It never builds up so it won't make surfaces slipperier, and it's nontoxic too! Call 1-800-528-3149 for a supplier near you.

CUSTOM CLEANER®: Try this if you're looking for a do-it-yourself dry-cleaning kit to freshen and spot-clean clothes. I love it. Custom Cleaner® works on all kinds of spots and has a very pleasant, clean scent. Look for this at grocery stores and discount stores.

DENATURED ALCOHOL: This is an industrial alcohol reserved for heavy-duty cleaning. Don't use it near an open flame, and make sure to dispose outside the home any rags that were used to apply it. Launder or clean anything that you treat with it as soon as possible. Look for this in cans at hardware stores and home centers.

DE-SOLV-IT CITRUS SOLUTION™: Available in home centers, hardware stores, etc., De-Solv-It Citrus-Solution™ has a multitude of uses both inside and out. Great for laundry.

ENERGINE CLEANING FLUID®: A great spotter. Look for this at the hardware store, the home center, and even in some grocery stores (usually on the top shelf with the laundry additives).

EPSOM SALTS: Usually used for medicinal

purposes, but handy for laundry too. Look for this in the drugstore.

EURONET USA: Makers of ACT Natural® Microfiber Cloths. These easy-to-use cloths have been scientifically proven to kill germs and bacteria. They even come with a warranty. I never travel without a cloth, and I keep one in my desk and briefcase to quickly clean up any of those little spills on clothes. Call 1-888-638-2882 or visit www.euronetusa.com

FELS-NAPTHA HEAVY-DUTY LAUNDRY BAR SOAP®: You'll find this wonderful laundry spotter and cleaner in the bar soap section of the grocery store. It's usually on the bottom shelf covered in dust, because nobody knows what to use it for!

FRESH BREEZE LAUNDRY SOAP®: See Soapworks.

GLYCERIN: Look for glycerin in drugstores in the hand cream section. Always purchase plain glycerin, *not* the type containing rosewater.

GOJO CRÈME WATERLESS HAND CLEANER®: Not just a hand cleaner, GOJO is great for laundry too. Look for it at home centers and hardware stores.

HYDROGEN PEROXIDE: Make sure to choose 3 percent—the type used for cuts, *not* the type used to bleach hair. (That's too strong and will remove color from fabric.)

MEAT TENDERIZER: Great for spotting protein stains. Use the unseasoned variety, please, or you will have a whole new stain to deal with. Store brands work fine.

NAIL POLISH REMOVER: I caution you to use non-acetone polish remover first. It's much less aggressive than acetone polish remover.

NONGEL TOOTHPASTE: This is just a fancy name for old-fashioned plain white toothpaste. Gels just don't work, so don't even try.

ODORZOUT®: A fabulous, dry, 100 percent natural deodorizer. It's nontoxic, so you can use it anyplace you have a smell or a stink. Also available in a pouch for shoes, laundry hampers, etc. Call 1-800-88STINK, or visit their website at www.88stink.com

PUREX® LAUNDRY DETERGENT: Available wherever detergents are sold.

RETAYNE®: Used *before* you launder colored clothes for the first time, it will help retain color. Available wherever quilting supplies are sold.

RUST REMOVER: These are serious products, so follow the directions carefully. Look for products like Whink® and Rust Magic® at hardware stores and home centers.

SHAVING CREAM: The cheaper brands work fine for spotting. Cream works better than gel.

SOAPWORKS®: Manufacturer of wonderful nontoxic, user-friendly and earth-friendly cleaning, laundry, and personal care products. Try their Fresh Breeze Laundry Powder®, originally designed for allergy and asthma sufferers. Also try their Brilliant Bleach™. Believe me, it *is* brilliant! Call 1-800-699-9917 or visit their website at www.soapworks.com

SOOT AND DIRT REMOVAL SPONGE: These big brick erasers are available at home centers and hardware stores, usually near the wallpaper supplies. Clean them by washing in a pail of warm water and liquid dish soap, rinse well, and allow to dry before using again.

SPOT SHOT INSTANT CARPET STAIN REMOVER®: My all-time favorite carpet spotter is a wonderful laundry spotter too! Available most everywhere, or call 1-800-848-4389.

SYNTHRAPOL®: Great for removing fugitive color. Available wherever quilting supplies are sold.

UN-DU™: Removes sticky residue from fabric and hard surfaces. Look for it at office supply, home centers and hardware stores.

WASHING SODA: I like Arm and Hammer® Washing Soda, which can be found in the detergent aisle at the grocery store along with other laundry additives. No, you cannot substitute baking soda; it's a different product!

WD-40 LUBRICANT®: Fine spray oil for lubricating all kinds of things, WD-40® is wonderful for regenerating grease so that it can be removed from clothes. Look for this at the hardware store, home center, and even the grocery store.

WIEMAN'S WAX AWAY™: Removes candle wax from fabrics and hard surfaces. Look for it at grocery stores and discount stores.

WINE AWAY RED WINE STAIN REMOVER™: This unbelievably good product can be found at Linens 'n Things, or wherever liquor is sold. Call 1-888-WINEAWAY for a store near you.

ZOUT STAIN REMOVER®: A very versatile laundry pre-spotter, Zout® is thicker than most laundry spotters, so you can target the spot. It really works! Buy it in grocery stores, discount stores, etc.